FARM MACHINES

TRACTOR

KATHY MIDDLETON

A Crabtree Roots Book

Crabtree Publishing
crabtreebooks.com

School-to-Home Support for Caregivers and Teachers

This book helps children grow by letting them practice reading. Here are a few guiding questions to help readers build comprehension skills. Possible answers appear here in red.

Before Reading:

- What do I think this book is about?
    - *I think this book is about tractors.*
    - *I think this book will talk about what jobs tractors do.*
- What do I want to learn about this topic?
    - *I want to learn about what tractors do.*
    - *I want to learn why tractors are important farm machines.*

During Reading:

- I wonder why...
    - *I wonder why farmers use tractors.*
    - *I wonder why tractors are needed on a farm.*
- What have I learned so far?
    - *I have learned that tractors have a hitch.*
    - *I have learned that tractors pulll, lift, and push heavy loads.*

After Reading:

- What details did I learn about this topic?
    - *I have learned that some other equipment can be attached to a tractor.*
    - *I learned that tractors are used to help with crops.*
- Read the book again and look for the vocabulary words.
    - *I see the words **tractor** on page 3 and the word **farm** on page 13. The other vocabulary words are found on page 14.*

This is a **tractor**.

Tractors pull, lift, and push heavy **loads**.

FENDT

Other equipment attaches to a tractor's **hitch**.

Farmers use tractors to help with **crops**.

Many tractors have four wheels.

Tractors do a lot of different jobs on a **farm**.

Word List

Sight Words

a	farmers	lot	this
and	heavy	of	to
attaches	help	on	use
different	is	other	with
do	jobs	pull	
equipment	lift	push	

Words to Know

crops

farm

hitch

loads

tractor

35 Words

This is a **tractor**.

Tractors pull, lift, and push heavy **loads**.

Other equipment attaches to a tractor's **hitch**.

Farmers use tractors to help with **crops**.

Many tractors have four wheels.

Tractors do a lot of different jobs on a **farm**.

FARM MACHINES TRACTOR

Written by: Kathy Middleton
Designed by: Under the Oaks Media
Proofreader: Crystal Sikkens
Production manager: Candice Campbell
Prepress technician: Katherine Kantor

Photographs: All images from Sutterstock

Crabtree Publishing

crabtreebooks.com 800-387-7650

In Canada: We acknowledge the financial support of the Government of Canada through the Canada Book Fund for our publishing activities.

Printed in the U.S.A./CP2025

Published in Canada
Crabtree Publishing
616 Welland Ave.
St. Catharines, Ontario
L2M 5V6

Published in the United States
Crabtree Publishing
347 Fifth Ave
Suite 1402-145
New York, NY 10016

Library and Archives Canada Cataloguing in Publication
Available at Library and Archives Canada

Library of Congress Cataloging-in-Publication Data
Available at the Library of Congress

Hardcover: 978-1-0398-8103-7
Paperback: 978-1-0398-8464-9
Ebook (pdf): 978-1-0398-8223-2
Epub: 978-1-0398-8343-7
Audio: 978-1-0398-8506-6
Read-Along: 978-1-0398-8548-6